max science primary

Student Book 1

DISCOVERING THROUGH ENQUIRY

PAT DOWER

SERIES EDITOR: **BOB KIBBLE**

CB081800

macmillan education

INTERNATIONAL CURRICULUM

Macmillan Education
4 Crinan Street
London N1 9XW
A division of Springer Nature Limited

Companies and representatives throughout the world

Student Book (print) ISBN 978-1-380-01015-5
Digital Student Pack (DSB) ISBN 978-1-380-02402-2
Student Bundle Pack ISBN (print and digital SB) 978-1-380-02404-6

Text © Pat Dower 2019
Design and illustration © Springer Nature Limited 2019

The author has asserted their right to be identified as the author of this work in accordance with the Copyright, Designs and Patents Act 1988.

First published 2019

All rights reserved. No part of this publication may be reproduced, stored in a retrieval system, or transmitted in any form or by any means, electronic, mechanical, photocopying, recording, or otherwise, without the prior written permission of the publishers.

Original design by EMC Design Ltd and Macmillan Education
Page make-up by Tek-Art Ltd
Illustrated by Magriet Brink pp 3, 13, 14, 22, 29, 37, 48, 53, 54, 58, 63, 65, 69, 71, 72, 79; Anna Hancock c/o Beehive Illustration pp 8, 23, 30, 41, 45, 52, 57, 60, 62, 76, 81; Daniel Limon c/o Beehive Illustration pp 16, 20, 26, 35, 43, 54, 55, 75, 83; Baz Rowell c/o Beehive Illustration pp 21, 25, 29, 37, 48, 70, 79, 82; Ricard Zaplana Ruiz c/o Beehive Illustration pp 7, 28, 33, 42, 51, 61, 70, 73, 74, 78, 86
Cover design by Sparks Publishing Services Ltd and Macmillan Education
Cover illustration by Star Publishing Pte Ltd and Jorge Santillan c/o Beehive Illustration Agency
Picture research by Susannah Jayes

The author and publishers would like to thank the following for permission to reproduce their photographs:

Alamy/art p22(cl), Alamy/Eric Gevaert p47(tr), Alamy/imageBROKER p72, Alamy/bob langrish p53; **Arava Institute for Environmental Studies** p84; **Brand X** p32; **Creatas** p39(cl); **DigitalVision** p44(br); **Getty Images** pp17(spatula, egg beater, grater), 19(cl), 20(br), Getty Images/Herman Agopia p4, Getty Images/Ingo Armdt p5(cl), Getty Images/artisteer p15, Getty Images/Martin Barraud p2, Getty Images/SandroBassi p22(bm), Getty Images/Blend Images p85, Getty Images/damircudic p66, Getty Images/Peter Dazeley p22(cr), Getty Images/dopma p17(chopping board), Getty Images/Dorling Kindersley p18(cl), Getty Images/Kevin Dyer p22(cml), Getty Images/Ekaterina79 p22(br), Getty Images/Marc Espolet Copyright p17(tablecloth), Getty Images/Fuse 9(bl), Getty Images/Andrej Giusgold p17(pots), Getty Images/Glasshouse Images p20(tr), Getty Images/Sharon Green p62, Getty Images/Patricia Hamilton pp27(tl), 77, Getty Images/VHammer p9(tr), Getty Images/ScottHughesPhotography p5(cm), Getty Images/Image Source p19(cr), Getty Images/iStockphoto/WLDavies p6(tr), Getty Images/iStockphoto/Thinkstock/Silfox p5(bm), Getty Images/iStockphoto/Thinkstock Images/thumb p59, Getty Images/jandielombard p57, Getty Images/joecicak p36, Getty Images/kali9 p63, Getty Images/Photos by R A Kearton p48, Getty Images/kissesfromholland p11(tr), Getty Images/Thomas Kokta p44(tr), Getty Images/Leelakajonkjj p87, Getty Images/Rob Lewine p30(cl), Getty Images/Sven Lobbert/EyeEm p47(cr), Getty Images/Mienny p59, Getty Images/Nature Picture Library p5(br), Getty Images/Mark Newman p38(t), Getty Images/David Papazian p20(br), Getty Images/Nigel Pavitt p10(tr), Getty Images/PBNJ Productions p12(tr), Getty Images/Anna Pekunova p11(bl), Getty Images/People Images p25, Getty Images/Taja Planinc p34(tr), Getty Images/MRodianova p27(br), Getty Images/Rudimencial p64, Getty Images/Lucas S p83, Getty Images/Stephen Scibetta/EyeEm p39(tr), Getty Images/Anup Shah/Minden Picturesp5(cr), Getty Images/Keren Su p6(br), Getty Images/Paul Taylor p21, Getty Images/tcsaba p50, Getty Images/Tetra Images – Rob Lewine p46, Getty Images/Tibourgartner p82, Getty Images/Stephen Trainoff Ph.D p5(bl), Getty Images/Richard Wahlstrom p38(b), Getty Images/Todd Warnock p49; **Image 100** p67(tr); **Jupiter Images** p18; **Photodisc** pp13, 47(cl); ©**Royalty-Free**/Corbis pp6(cl), 35(tr), 40; **Shutterstock**/Arcansel p27(tr), Shutterstock/Andrew Buckin p27(tm), Shutterstock/Emilio100 p88, Shutterstock/Dmitri Gomon p6(bl), Shutterstock/HiSunnySky p79, Shutterstock/Icrms p34(br), Shutterstock/katatonia82 p22(tr), Shutterstock/KOO p68, Shutterstock/Aleksei Lazukov p24, Shutterstock/Marketa Mark p39, Shutterstock/Monkey Business Images pp3, 12(br), Shutterstock/Sergey Novikov p80, Shutterstock/PhotoAlto p67(br), Shutterstock/ruzanna p22(cm), Shutterstock/Sergey0506 p22(bl), Shutterstock/Kuttelvaserova Stuchelova p11(tm), Shutterstock/tratong p10(br), Shutterstock/Peter Vanco p35(tm), Shutterstock/wavebreakmedia p7.

These materials may contain links for third party websites. We have no control over, and are not responsible for, the contents of such third party websites. Please use care when accessing them.

The inclusion of any specific companies, commercial products, trade names or otherwise, does not constitute or imply its endorsement or recommendation by Springer Nature Limited.

Printed and bound in Brazil

2024
21

Contents

Introducing *Max Science primary*

Max Science primary is a science course designed to meet the needs of learners following the Cambridge International Primary curriculum framework for Stages 1 to 6.

Success in science learning for young international learners and their teachers is enhanced through its practical approach to the skills of scientific enquiry and scientific vocabulary. Investigation and language activities in each unit progress learners from simple to more complex to make learning and understanding science accessible and fun.

The **Student Books** guide learners through key scientific knowledge, language and skills in the Cambridge curriculum. Each unit begins with an engaging introduction followed by activities that introduce and reinforce the skills of scientific enquiry providing opportunities for learners to develop subject knowledge through investigation.

The **Workbooks** expand the key activities in each unit for use by the learners in pairs and groups in the classroom, or as individuals at home.

To further support the course, each stage has a **Journal** for use by learners at home, with the support of adults, to reinforce the knowledge and language of each topic. Teachers can review Journals at different points throughout the term to check progress at home against progress in school.

Also available are ***Max Science primary* Digital Student Books**, which offer an accompaniment to the more traditional printed Student Books. Ideal for encouraging digital literacy, these online books mirror the print course while offering extra interactive activities and assessment opportunities at home or in class.

Student Book features

Unit openers

Introduce the unit with clearly defined learning objectives, and stimulate interest with starter questions and images.

Orientation

Starter activities engage learners and help teachers assess how much the class already knows, before exploring further.

Key words

Key words for each section are clearly shown.

Interesting facts

Link science in the classroom to science in the real world.

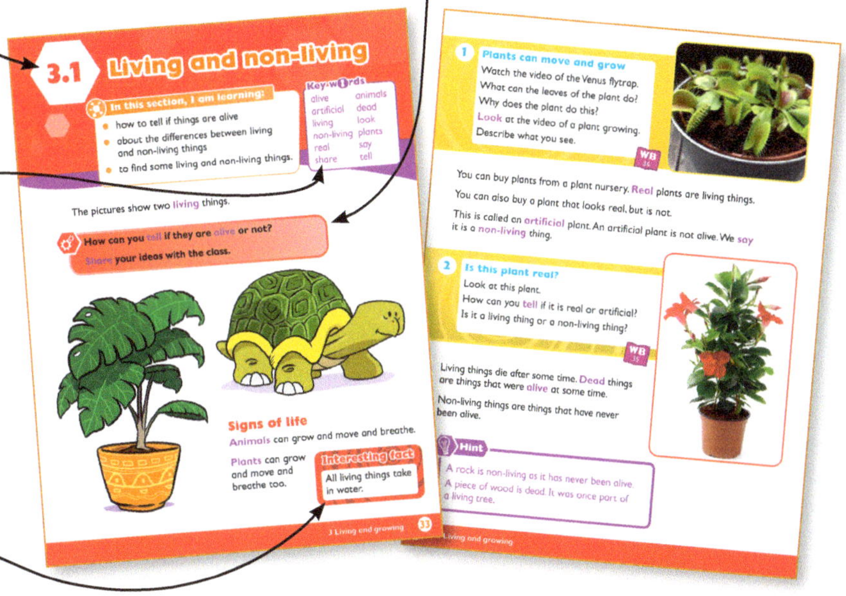

3.1 Living and non-living

In this section, I am learning:
- how to tell if things are alive
- about the differences between living and non-living things
- to find some living and non-living things.

Key words: alive, artificial, living, non-living, real, share, animals, dead, look, plants, say, tell

The pictures show two living things.

How can you tell if they are alive or not? Share your ideas with the class.

Signs of life

Animals can grow and move and breathe.

Plants can grow and move and breathe too.

Interesting fact: All living things take in water.

3 Living and growing 33

1 Plants can move and grow

Watch the video of the Venus flytrap. What can the leaves of the plant do? Why does the plant do this? Look at the video of a plant growing. Describe what you see.

You can buy plants from a plant nursery. Real plants are living things. You can also buy a plant that looks real, but is not. This is called an artificial plant. An artificial plant is not alive. We say it is a non-living thing.

2 Is this plant real?

Look at this plant. How can you tell if it is real or artificial? Is it a living thing or a non-living thing?

Living things die after some time. Dead things are things that were alive at some time. Non-living things are things that have never been alive.

Hint: A rock is non-living as it has never been alive. A piece of wood is dead. It was once part of a living tree.

Living and growing

Exploring science

Investigations and extension questions help develop skills and understanding, and enable learners to explore, test, measure, record, interpret and predict scientific questions.

Workbook icon

Workbook icons in the Student Book direct teachers and learners to the corresponding activities in the workbook.

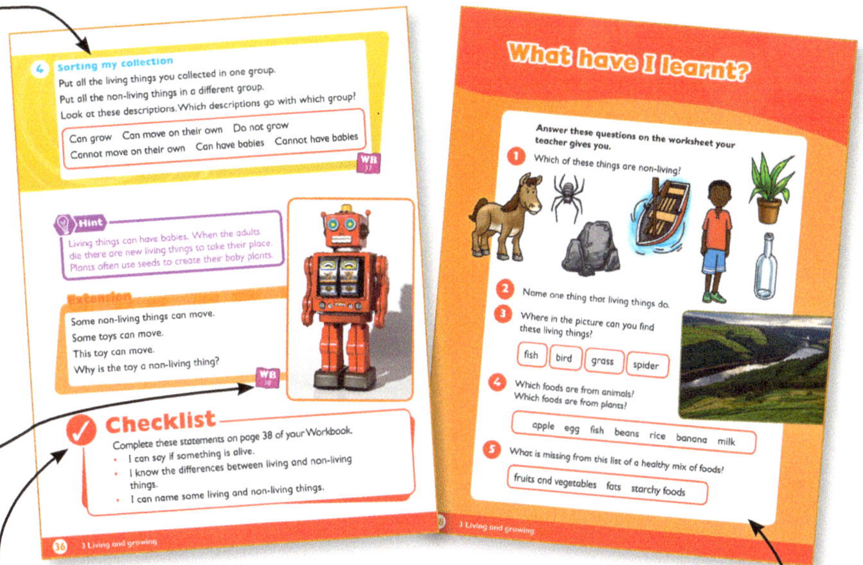

4 Sorting my collection

Put all the living things you collected in one group. Put all the non-living things in a different group. Look at these descriptions. Which descriptions go with which group?

Can grow · Can move on their own · Do not grow · Cannot move on their own · Can have babies · Cannot have babies

Hint: Living things can have babies. When the adults die there are new living things to take their place. Plants often use seeds to create their baby plants.

Extension: Some non-living things can move. Some toys can move. This toy can move. Why is the toy a non-living thing?

Checklist

Complete these statements on page 38 of your Workbook.
- I can say if something is alive.
- I know the differences between living and non-living things.
- I can name some living and non-living things.

36 3 Living and growing

What have I learnt?

Answer these questions on the worksheet your teacher gives you.

1 Which of these things are non-living?

2 Name one thing that living things do.

3 Where in the picture can you find these living things? fish · bird · grass · spider

4 Which foods are from animals? Which foods are from plants? apple · egg · fish · beans · rice · banana · milk

5 What is missing from this list of a healthy mix of foods? fruits and vegetables · fats · starchy foods

3 Living and growing

Assessing progress

End of topic checklists allow learners to check what they have learnt so far.

Cambridge Primary curriculum framework

In the spirit of the Cambridge Primary curriculum checkpoint tests, end of unit activities ask 'what have I learnt?' to sum up where learners have got to in their learning journey so far.*

*See *also* the online versions at www.macmillaneducationeverywhere.com for downloading and printing with complete answer spaces provided.

1 Ourselves

In this unit, I am learning:

- how we are the same
- how we are different
- the parts of the human body
- how we use our five senses
- how senses tell us about our surroundings
- how animals use their senses.

Key words

animal
body
different
human
same
senses

What are humans like?

Draw a picture of a person. Can you say or write the names of the parts of the body?

1.1 The human body

In this section, I am learning:

- how we are the same
- how we are different.

Key words

animals
body
comparing
different
find
grow
humans
look
mammals
move
same
similar

Work with a partner.
Stand up and look at each other.

What is the same?

What is different?

Share your answers with the rest of the class.

Extension

Find out more things about your partner.

Can you both **move**?
Can you both run?

Do you both **grow**?
Are you the same height?

Tick the answers in your Workbook.

WB

How humans are different

Humans are all the **same** in some ways.

Humans are also all **different** in some ways.

Look at the children in this picture.

Each child's **body** has two arms, two legs and a head.

One has dark hair. The other has light hair.

One is taller than the other.

1 My features

What colour are your eyes?

What colour is your hair?

What size are your shoes?

Make a class chart.

WB 1

Humans all have **similar** bodies.

Some of our features are different.

2 Comparing children in my class

Look at the class chart you made earlier.

Find things that are the same.

Find things that are different.

WB 2

Hint

When you can find things that are the same and things that are different, this is called **comparing**.

Humans and **animals** are the same in some ways.

Some of their features are similar.

Humans and animals can also use their bodies in similar ways.

human

Extension

Get into groups. Look at the animal pictures.

How are the animals the same as humans?

How are the animals different from humans?

Tick the answers in your Workbook.

WB 2

ape

grasshopper

cat

fish

bird

spider

Which features do you think all humans have?

Interesting fact

Humans belong to a group of animals called **mammals**.

You are a mammal.

Lions, elephants, camels and goats are all mammals.

3 Sorting human features

Find a partner.

Take it in turns to choose a feature.

Sort the features into three groups.

WB 3

1.2 Parts of the human body

In this section, I am learning:

- the parts of the human body.

Key words

arms, ears, eyes, feet, fingers, hair, hands, head, knees, legs, mouth, nose, say, shoulders, toes

Which parts of the body can you say?

Body parts

Your **head** has your **nose**, **ears**, **eyes** and **mouth** on it.

Below your head, your body has **shoulders**, **arms** and **legs**.

Your arms have **hands** and **fingers**.

Your legs have **knees**, **feet** and **toes**.

1 The body song

With your teacher, sing:
"Head, shoulders, knees and toes".

Sing it until you know it.

How many body parts are in the song?

WB 4

2 Draw and label the body

Work in a group.

One of you lies down on a big sheet of paper.

Now draw around the person.

Label the body parts.

Now look at other groups' labels.

Do you want to change any of yours?

WB 4

Extension

Add these extra labels to the body outline you made:

neck, hip, waist, finger, eyelash, mouth

WB 5

Interesting fact

A giraffe is an animal, just like a human.

It has a head, neck, legs, eyes and **hair**.

A giraffe is taller than three men.

Is any animal taller than a giraffe?

Checklist

Complete these statements on page 6 of your Workbook.

- I can say how humans are the same.
- I can say how humans can be different.
- I can name parts of the human body.

1.3 Sensing

In this section, I am learning:

- how we use our five senses
- how senses tell us about our surroundings
- how animals use their senses.

Key words

feel, guess, hear, hearing, see, senses, show, sight, smell, taste, touch

How do you learn about the world around you?

Five senses

Humans have five **senses**.

They are **hearing**, **sight**, **smell**, **taste** and **touch**.

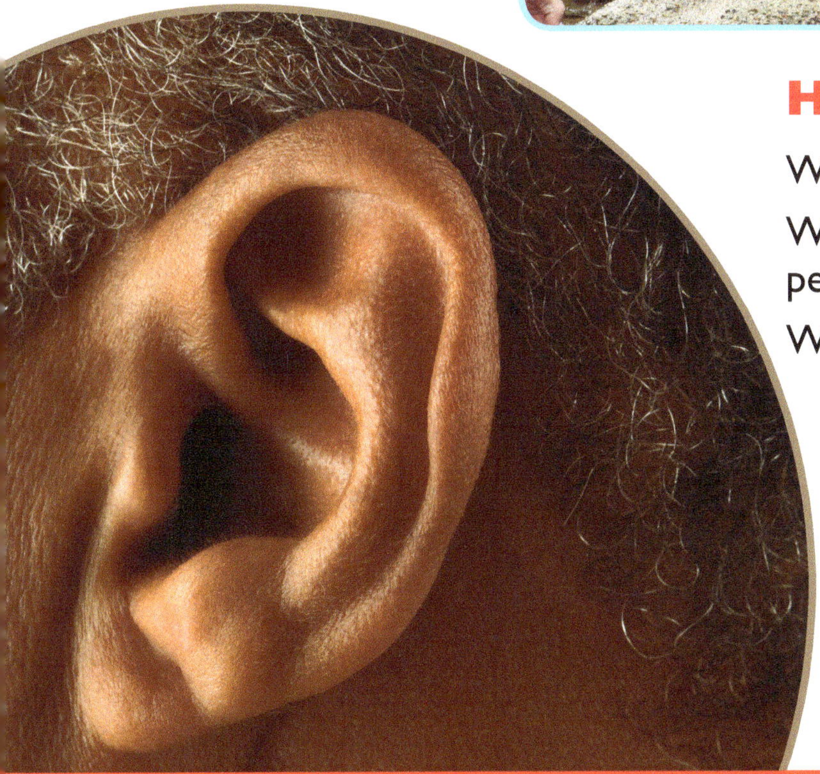

Hearing

We use our ears to **hear** sound.

We use our ears to hear people talk.

We use our ears to listen to music.

Hint

To listen, you have to pay attention to the sounds you hear.

1 Hearing

Close your eyes. Listen to the sounds your teacher will make.

Can you tell what each sound is?

Your teacher will **show** you what is making each sound.

WB 7

Animals can use their ears to listen for danger.

Sight

We use our eyes to **see**.

Most animals have eyes too.

2 The "I spy…" game

Work with a partner.

One of you looks around the room and chooses an object. Don't say what it is.

Say the rhyme: "I spy, with my little eye, something beginning with…"

The other person **guesses** the word.

Now swap round.

WB 8

Smell

We use our noses to **smell**.

Some animals find food by smelling.

3 Do you know the smell?

Work with a partner. Wear a blindfold. Can you tell what the smell is?

What is your favourite smell?

WB 9

Taste

You can taste things in your mouth.

We use words like "sour" or "sweet" to describe different tastes.

A lemon tastes sour. Chocolate is sweet.

4 Guess the food

Work with a partner.

One of you wears a blindfold.

The other feeds a bit of food to the person with the blindfold.

Can you guess what the food is?

WB 10

Touch and feeling

You can **feel** things on your skin.

You can feel things with your hands.

5 **What is in the box?**

Feel the object in the box.

What does it feel like?

Do you know what it is? Don't tell.

WB 11

We can use more than one sense to find out about something.

Sometimes one sense is more important than another.

Which sense is most important for music?

6 Name the senses

Your teacher will do five things.

Point to the body part you are using to sense each one.

Write the words for the senses in your Workbook.

WB 12

ringing a bell

shining a light

beating a drum

holding a balloon

switching on a fan

What would life be like if one of your senses did not work?

Interesting fact

Some animals have better senses than others.

A bird of prey can see eight times more clearly than a human.

Checklist

Complete these statements on page 13 of your Workbook.

- I can say what the five senses do.
- I can say what my senses tell me about my surroundings.
- I can say how humans and animals use senses.

What have I learnt?

Answer these questions on the worksheet your teacher gives you.

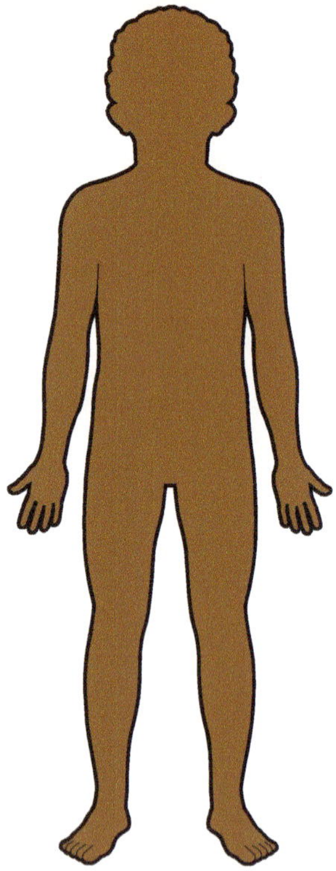

1. Look at the picture of the person. Point to where these parts of your body are.

head	shoulder	leg	foot

2. You have five senses. Which two are missing from this list?

sight	touch	smell

3. Which are the animals?

4. Say which word completes each sentence correctly:

eyes	skin	taste	smell

We use our ____ to see. We use our nose to ____.

We use our mouth to ____. We use our ____ to feel things.

2 What is it made of?

Key words
different
job
material
object
properties
sort

In this unit, I am learning:

- what a material is
- about different materials
- to name different materials
- words to describe what materials are like
- what some materials are used for
- how materials are used for different jobs
- to suggest good materials to use for different jobs
- different ways to sort materials
- how the properties of materials help us sort them.

Look around your classroom. What objects can you see?

2.1 Exploring materials with my senses

In this section, I am learning:

- what a material is
- about different materials.

Key words

choose, fabric, material, object, properties, wood, draw, look, metal, plastic, say

What do you think the word "material" means?

Our clothes are made from **fabric**. Another word for fabric is "**material**".

Look at what the **objects** in the pictures are made from.

The pencil is made from **wood**.

The cutlery is made from **metal**.

The blocks are made from **plastic**.

These objects are made from different materials.

So, a material is what something is made from.

1 Talking about materials

Get into pairs. **Choose** some objects from around the room.

Look at the materials the objects are made of. Touch the materials.

Are the objects all made from the same materials?

Take it in turns to tell your partner about each material.

Write about two materials in your Workbook.

WB 16

Some objects are made from more than one material.

Extension

Look at these objects from a kitchen.

spatula

tablecloth

egg beater

chopping board

grater

pots

What materials do you see?

Which objects are made from more than one material?

Draw one of these objects in your Workbook.

WB 17

Different materials

Everything is made from materials.

Metal is a material.

Plastic is a material.

Fabric is a material.

2 **Finding materials**

Look for materials that belong to you.

How many materials can you find in one minute?

In your Workbook, circle the materials you found.

WB 17

Materials have **properties**.

They can be hard. They can be soft. Those are properties.

We can use our senses to describe a material's properties.

3 **Using my sense of touch**

Your teacher will give you some bags. Feel the outside of each bag. What is the material like?

Put your hand inside each bag. What is the object?

What is the material it is made from like?

Can you **say** what the material is?

WB 18

Interesting fact

Plastic is a material made by humans. Wood is a material from nature.

2.2 What are materials like?

In this section, I am learning:

- to name different materials
- words to describe what materials are like
- what some materials are used for.

Key words

bendy
find out
hard
polystyrene
soft
strong
write
compare
glass
paper
rubber
stone
waterproof

In pairs, compare the spoon and the scissors.

- **What material are they made from?**
- **What other materials can a spoon be made from?**
- **Can scissors be made from another material?**

Explain what you think.

Talk to another group about your answer.

Comparing materials

We can **compare** materials by describing their properties.

Glass is see-through.

Fabric is **soft**.

You can squash **rubber**.

Metal is **hard** and **strong**.

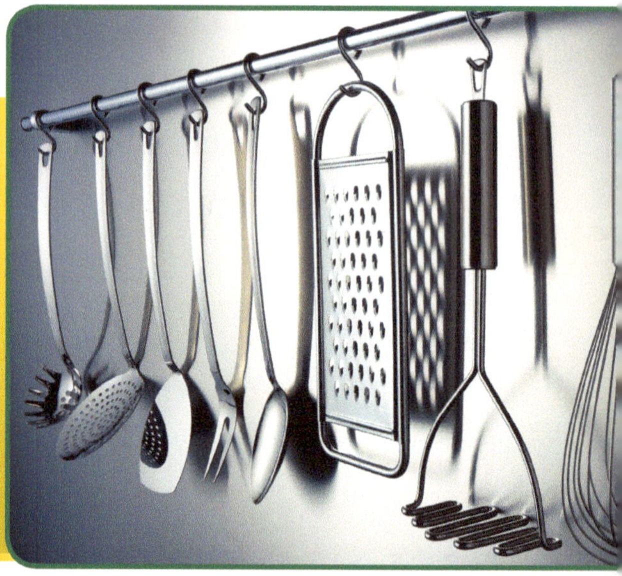

1 Properties of metal

Look at these objects made from metal.

Which of these words describe metal?

soft hard strong breakable
smooth rough **bendy**

WB 19

2 Properties of wood

Look at the picture. These planks are made from wood.

Which of these words describe wood?

soft hard strong breakable
smooth rough bendy

WB 19

Extension

What other words describe metal?
What other words describe wood?

WB 19

Glass and plastic

Some bottles are made from glass.

Some bottles are made from plastic.

3 Guessing materials

Get into pairs. Look at the bottles and jars.

What materials are they made of?

Tell your partner.

Why are these good materials for bottles?

WB 20

4 Musical bottles

Akim wants to make a musical instrument using bottles.

He can make music-like sounds by tapping the bottles.

Predict which material is better – plastic or glass.

Do a test to **find out**.

WB 20

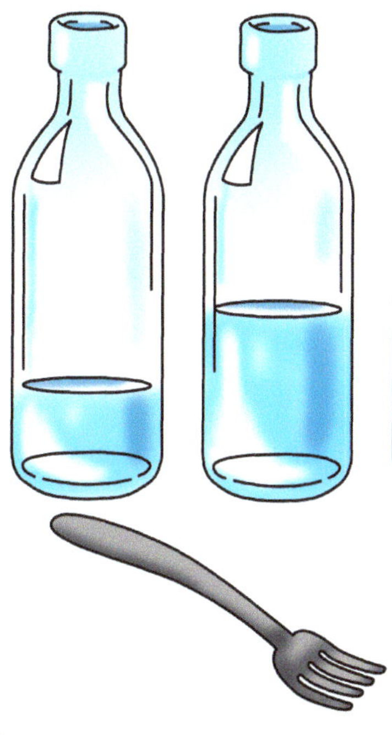

Materials have useful properties.

We use materials to solve problems.

5 Solving problems

Choose one of these problems:

1 Keeping firewood out of the rain.

2 Making a cat bed.

3 Keeping picnic food cool on a hot day.

4 Mopping up water on the floor.

Which material can you use to solve the problem?

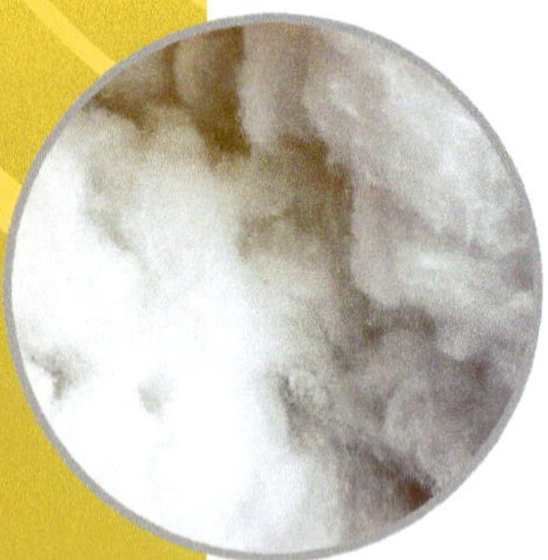

Why did you choose the material?

WB 21

Hint

Using two materials makes this girl's coat warm and **waterproof**.

Finding and naming more materials

This bridge is made of **stone**.

The tyre is made of rubber.

This cup is made of **polystyrene**.

Books are made of **paper**.

6 Comparing materials

Look around your school. Find different objects made from each of the materials in the four pictures.

In your Workbook, draw one object made from each of the materials.

Write the names of the objects.

How many different objects did you find made from each material?

WB 22

Checklist

Complete these statements on page 23 of your Workbook.

- I can say what a material is.
- I can name at least five different materials.
- I can use words to describe different materials.
- I can give examples of what the materials are used for.

2.3 Understanding materials

In this section, I am learning:

- how materials are used for different jobs
- to suggest good materials to use for different jobs.

Key words

ask
foam
job
metal
nylon
share
show

The picture is of a parachute made of **nylon**. It is very light and strong.

Can you think of other materials that are light?

Can you think of materials that are strong?

Exploring words to describe materials

You have already used different words to describe the properties of materials.

For example, a property of wool is that it is soft.

A property of **metal** is that it is strong.

Here are some more words to describe the properties of materials:

hard heavy light stretchy smooth shiny

What other words can you think of?

1 **Spotting different materials**

Get into pairs.

How many different materials can you see in the picture?

Ask a partner what they see.

WB 24

2 **Finding materials with specific properties**

Play this game outside.

Your teacher will say: "Find a soft material!"

Run to a soft material and put your hand on it.

Do this for other properties such as hard, shiny, bendy.

WB 25

Choosing materials for different jobs

Look at this bicycle. It is made of many different materials.

Each material does a specific **job**.

Using materials in interesting ways

We choose materials for certain jobs because of the material's properties.

3 Materials for a house

Get into groups.

What job does each part of the house do?

Which properties does each part of the house need?

Talk about this question in your group.

Write the words on the picture in your Workbook.

WB 25

Materials do many different things.

4 What can materials do?

Your teacher will **show** you some objects. They are made from specific materials. Get into pairs.

How do the material's properties help each object to do its job?

- Think by yourself.
- Tell your partner.
- **Share** your ideas with the class.

Record them in your Workbook.

WB 26

Interesting fact

Houses in different places are built from different materials. People use materials that are easy to get and can do the right job.

Extension

Step 1:

Make two small balls out of modelling clay.

Hold one ball up high and then drop it.

Look at the ball.

What has happened to the ball?

Step 2:

Foam is a soft material.

Wrap the second ball in foam.

Hold it up high and drop it.

What has happened to the ball?

WB 27

2.4 Sorting materials

In this section, I am learning:

- different ways to sort materials
- how the properties of materials help us sort them.

Key words

different group guess sort

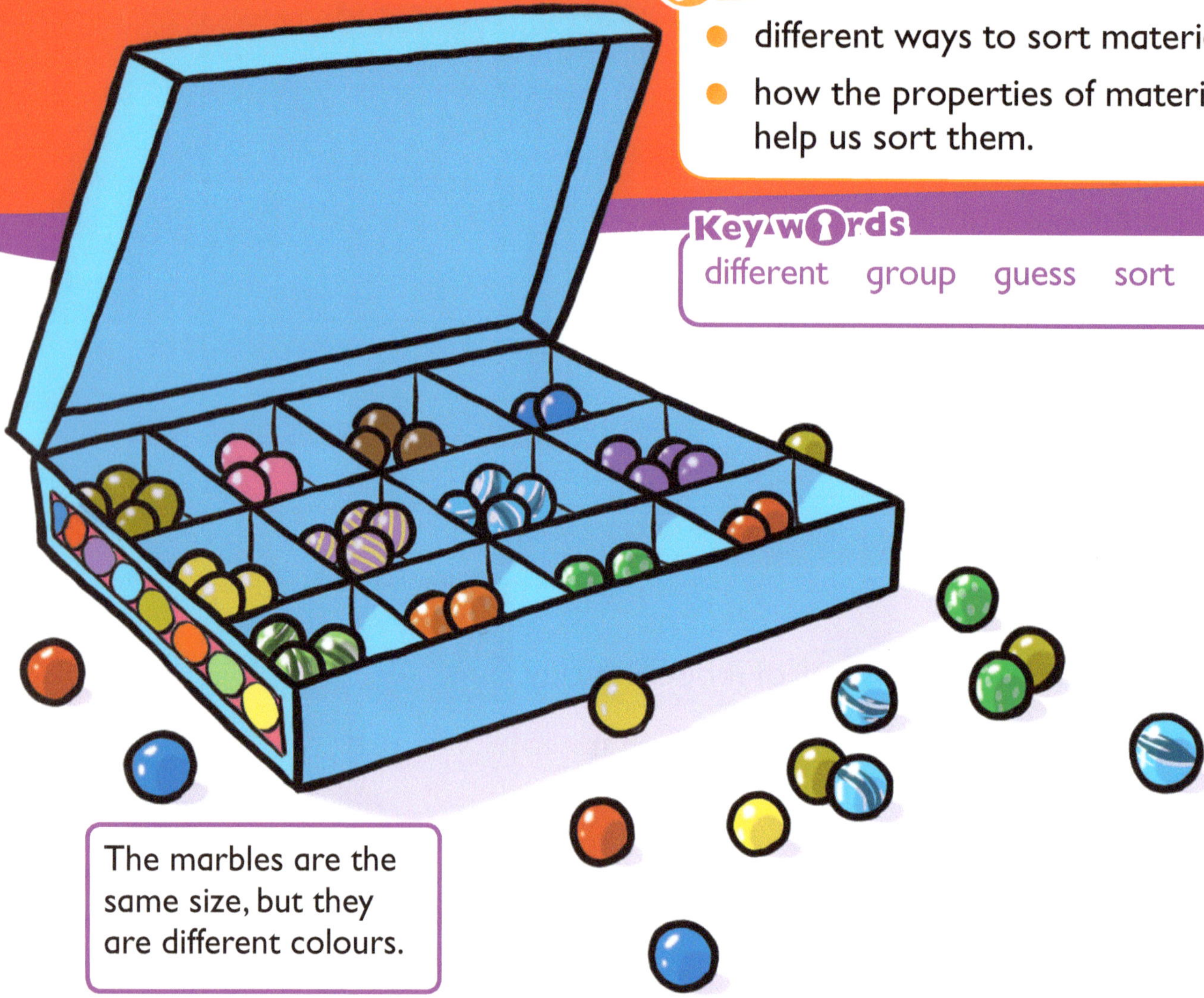

The marbles are the same size, but they are different colours.

There are different ways to sort things.

How can you sort these buttons?

How can we sort materials?

Materials have **different** properties.

We can use properties to **sort** materials.

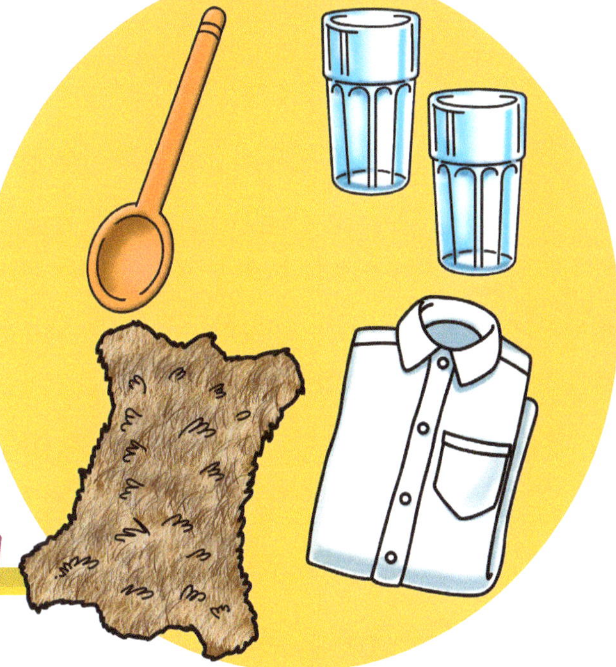

1 Sorting into groups

Sort these objects into two **groups**.

Draw and name your sorted materials in your Workbook.

WB 28

2 Making a sorting poster

Choose up to ten materials and sort them into two groups.

You can choose from this list:

stone, **metal**, **wood**, **plastic**, **fur**, **wool**, **cotton**, **rubber**, **paper**, **leather**.

Use the properties of the materials to group them.

Make a poster.

Stick your materials onto the poster or draw pictures.

Label the properties you used.

WB 29

Hint

There are different ways to sort things. For example:

- hard or soft
- shiny or dull
- strong or weak
- slippery or not slippery.

3 Properties game

Get into groups. Make a set of cards.

Write the name of a material on one side of each card.

On the other side, write the material's properties and uses.

Play a game to **guess** materials from their descriptions.

Look in the Workbook for the rules of the game.

WB 29

Extension

What materials are best for making a bicycle?

What materials are best for making a sofa?

Sort them in your Workbook.

WB 30

Checklist

Complete these statements on page 31 of your Workbook.

- I can explain how materials are used for different jobs.
- I can suggest good materials to use for different jobs.
- I can sort materials in different ways.
- I can use the properties of materials to help me sort them.

What have I learnt?

Answer these questions on the worksheet your teacher gives you.

1. What materials are used to make a bicycle?
2. What material can bottles be made from?
3. Look at the table below. Which properties match each material?

Metal	• Hard • Strong • Soft
Wood	• Hard • Strong • Soft
Glass	• Hard • Strong • Soft

4. Sort these materials into two groups. What properties did you use?

nylon stone glass metal polystyrene

3 Living and growing

In this unit, I am learning:

- how to tell if things are alive
- about the differences between living and non-living things
- to find some living and non-living things
- where plants live
- where animals live
- where foods come from
- about healthy things to eat and drink
- about baby animals, including humans.

Key words

alive
animals
healthy
living
non-living
plants
young

What can you see in this picture?

What do you want to ask about the picture?

Your teacher will keep your questions for later.

3.1 Living and non-living

In this section, I am learning:

- how to tell if things are alive
- about the differences between living and non-living things
- to find some living and non-living things.

Key words

alive	animals
artificial	dead
living	look
non-living	plants
real	say
share	tell

The pictures show two **living** things.

How can you tell if they are alive or not?

Share your ideas with the class.

Signs of life

Animals can grow and move and breathe.

Plants can grow and move and breathe too.

Interesting fact

All living things take in water.

1 Plants can move and grow

Watch the video of the Venus flytrap.

What can the leaves of the plant do?

Why does the plant do this?

Look at the video of a plant growing.

Describe what you see.

WB 34

You can buy plants from a plant nursery. **Real** plants are living things.

You can also buy a plant that looks real, but is not.

This is called an **artificial** plant. An artificial plant is not alive. We **say** it is a **non-living** thing.

2 Is this plant real?

Look at this plant.

How can you **tell** if it is real or artificial?

Is it a living thing or a non-living thing?

WB 35

Living things die after some time. **Dead** things are things that were **alive** at some time.

Non-living things are things that have never been alive.

Hint

A rock is non-living as it has never been alive.

A piece of wood is dead. It was once part of a living tree.

Extension

Look at these pictures. Which one is the real baby?

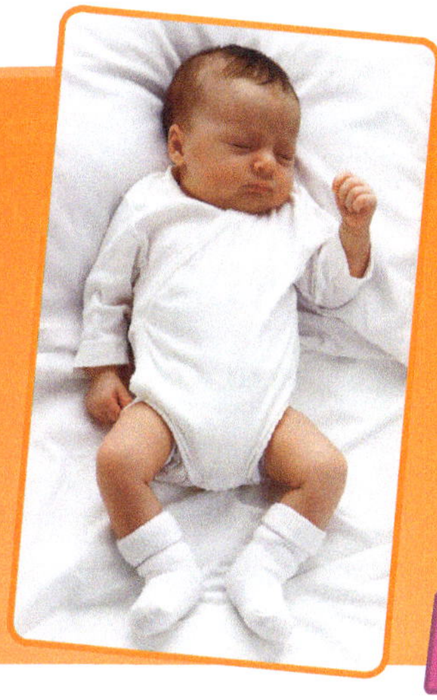

WB 36

Living things can move on their own.

Living things grow.

3 Finding living and non-living things

Work in a pair.

Go on a walk around the school grounds.

Take a bag and collect examples of living and non-living things.

Take pictures of what you collect.

Do not harm any living things.

WB 36

4 Sorting my collection

Put all the living things you collected in one group.

Put all the non-living things in a different group.

Look at these descriptions. Which descriptions go with which group?

Can grow | Can move on their own | Do not grow
Cannot move on their own | Can have babies | Cannot have babies

WB 37

Hint

Living things can have babies. When the adults die there are new living things to take their place. Plants often use seeds to create their baby plants.

Extension

Some non-living things can move.

Some toys can move.

This toy can move.

Why is the toy a non-living thing?

WB 38

Checklist

Complete these statements on page 38 of your Workbook.

- I can say if something is alive.
- I know the differences between living and non-living things.
- I can name some living and non-living things.

3.2 Living things around me

In this section, I am learning:

- where plants live
- where animals live.

Key words

ask
compare
dry
cold
damp

Look at the pictures.

Where do you think you will find many living things?

Looking for life

Plants and animals need certain things to live. Without these things, they will die

1 Staying alive

Look at Picture A.

What do living things need to live?

Circle the words in your Workbook.

Picture A

Now look at Picture B.

Picture B

Why can things not live here?

WB 39

2 Outside learning walk

Your teacher will take you on a learning walk.

How many different plants can you see?

How many different animals can you see?

WB 40

Where things live

Look at the pictures.

I live in **cold** places.

I live in **damp** places.

I live in **dry** places where there is very little water.

3 What is it like where you live?

Talk about your answers in a group.

WB 40

4 Looking in other places

Your teacher will show you a video.

How many different plants and animals can you see?

What is it like where they live?

Talk about your answers in a group.

Compare this place with what you saw on your learning walk.

WB 41

Hint

Different plants and animals prefer different places to live.

Extension

What is your favourite wild animal?

Ask your partner what their favourite wild animal is.

WB 42

Checklist

Complete these statements on page 43 of your Workbook.

- I can say where some plants live.
- I can say where some animals live.

3.3 Eating to live

In this section, I am learning:

- where foods come from
- about healthy things to eat and drink.

Key words

drink, eat, foods, food groups, guess, healthy, water

People need to **eat** many different **foods** to stay **healthy**.

What are your favourite foods?

Look at the picture.

Foods can be sorted into:

- foods that come from plants
- foods that come from animals.

A healthy mix of foods

Foods can be sorted into **food groups.**

Look at the picture. To grow up healthy you need to eat food from all these groups.

Fruit and vegetables help you to stay well.

Starchy foods help you to run and play.

Meat, fish, eggs and dairy help you to grow strong and tall.

Fats help to keep your brain healthy and cushion your organs against bumps.

1 Grouping foods

Choose some foods from those your teacher wrote down.

Which group would you put them in?

Match the foods to their group in your Workbook.

WB 44

2 Food posters

Make class posters for each food group.

WB 45

Drinking

You must have **water** to stay alive.

Fresh, clean water is the best thing to **drink**.

Juice and fizzy drinks have sugar in them.

Too much sugar is bad for your teeth.

3 Sugar in drinks

Watch what happens when a spoon of sugar is stirred into water.

Can you see the sugar?

Your teacher will show you a drink.

Guess how many spoons of sugar are in the drink.

Your teacher will show how many spoons of sugar are in the drink.

Interesting fact

You cannot always see what is in food and drinks!

WB 45

Eating the right mix of food helps us stay healthy.

Extension

Look again at the diagram on the previous page.
What foods do you eat most?
What types of food should you eat only a little bit of?

WB 46

✓ Checklist

Complete these statements on page 46 of your Workbook.

- I can say where different foods come from.
- I can name healthy things to eat.
- I can say what is healthy to drink.

3.4 Baby animals

In this section, I am learning:

- about baby animals, including humans.

Key words

answer, family, farm, generation, human, pet, young

Look at the picture.

What do the parents do for the baby penguin?

Animals and their young

Adult animals give birth to baby animals.

Baby animals are called **young**. They are also called "offspring".

The young animals grow up into adults.

1 Spotting the mistake

Look at the pictures in your Workbook.

Spot the mistake.

WB 47

Naming young animals

Some young animals have special names. For example:
Young cats are called kittens. A cat is a **pet**.
Pets are animals you keep at home.
Young goats are called kids. A goat is a **farm** animal.
Farm animals give us things like milk and eggs.

2 Matching animals and their young

Match the young farm animals with their mothers in your Workbook.

WB 48

3 Pets and farm animals

Pick one animal.
What do you think the animal was like when it was a baby?
Pick one from each pair of words:

The baby was [bigger smaller] than its mother.

The baby was [weaker stronger] than its mother.

What else do you think was different?

WB 49

Human young

A fully grown animal is called an adult.

A **human** baby takes a long time to become an adult.

4 Young humans

How old are you?
How old will you be when you become an adult?

WB 49

Human families

In a **family**, children, parents and grandparents can all be alive at the same time. Some families have great-grandparents as well.

Each group is called a **generation**. Children are one generation. Parents are another generation.

How many generations can you see in this family picture?

5 Human families quiz

Tell your partner about your family.
Who is the oldest?
Who is the youngest?
How many are female?
How many are male?
Are there any babies on the way?
How many generations are alive in your family?

WB 50

Hint

Generations have names:

child → parent → grandparent → great-grandparent

Interesting fact

Humans are mammals.

All baby mammals feed on their mothers' milk.

6 **Starting questions**

As a class, try to **answer** your questions from the beginning of this unit.

WB 51

Checklist

Complete these statements on page 51 of your Workbook.

- I can compare young animals with their parents.
- I know that families have groups called generations.

What have I learnt?

Answer these questions on the worksheet your teacher gives you.

1. Which of these things are non-living?

2. Name one thing that living things do.

3. Where in the picture can you find these living things?

   fish | bird | grass | spider

4. Which foods are from animals?
   Which foods are from plants?

   apple egg fish beans rice banana milk

5. What is missing from this list of a healthy mix of foods?

   fruits and vegetables fats starchy foods

4 Pushes and pulls

In this unit, I am learning:

- to see different kinds of movement
- to name different kinds of movement
- about forces
- that pushes and pulls are kinds of force
- to see changes in movement
- what makes movement change.

Key words

cause
force
movement
pull
push

Look at the picture. What is happening?

How many different types of movement can you see?

4.1 Moving

In this section, I am learning:

- to see different kinds of movement
- to name different kinds of movement.

Key words

fast find
jump look
move, moving
movement
show slow
swing talk about
turn write

Work with a partner. Look around you. Find five things that move. Which words can you think of to say how these things move?

1 How does it move?

Look at the toy in the picture.

Also look at the toy your teacher shows you.

What are the toys doing? In your group, **talk about** what you see.

Choose three words to describe what you see.

WB 54

Types of movement

These living things are all **moving**.

This rabbit is **hopping.**

This person is **running.**

This boy is **swimming.**

This caterpillar is **crawling.**

2 PE drum game

Work in a large space.

Walk around the space and do these actions when you hear the drum:

One drum beat – **jump** up and then carry on walking.

Two drum beats – **turn** around and then carry on walking.

Three drum beats – **swing** your arms and then carry on walking.

Think of your own actions and **write** them in your Workbook.

WB 54

Look at the boy's footsteps. They **show** that he is walking in a circle.

Carry out this action.

Do it **slow**.

Do it **fast**.

Does going fast make the movement easier or more difficult? Why do you say so?

3 Things move in many ways

These things can all **move**:

snail car aeroplane frog

Find two words from the box to describe how each one moves.

fast slow turn fly jump slide
crawl spin up down glide

Try to find one more word for each thing.

WB 55

4 What movement is this?

Watch the video clip of a hamster on a wheel. What kind of **movement** is it?

What other things move like the hamster wheel?

In a group, see how many different things you can think of.

WB 55

Hint

Wheels go round.
Wheels on a bicycle go round.

Sports

What kinds of movement can you see in these pictures?

Choose from:

turning swinging jumping punching
hitting rising falling stretching running

WB 56

Interesting fact

Humans take a year or more to learn to walk.

Horses can walk a few hours after being born.

Checklist

Complete these statements on page 57 of your Workbook.

- I can spot different types of movement.
- I can name at least three different types of movement.

4.2 Push and pull

In this section, I am learning:

- about forces
- that pushes and pulls are kinds of force.

Key words

answer
compare
draw
force
predict
pull
push

Look at these pictures.

Which show a push?

Which show a pull?

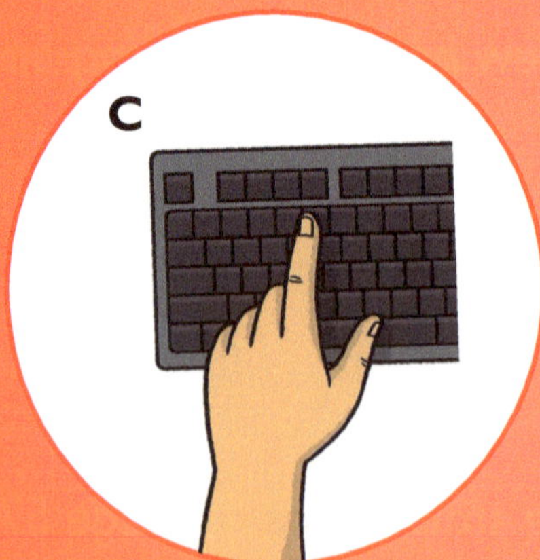

Forces

This car is standing still.
A **push** can make it move.

A push is a kind of **force**.

A push moves things further away. It can also change their direction.

A **pull** is another kind of force.

A pull brings things closer. It can change their direction too.

1 Which force?

This picture shows a shopping trolley.

Which force is needed to move the trolley forwards?

Which force is needed to move the trolley backwards?

WB 58

Turning forces

How can you open this bottle?

2 Turning

Look at the six objects in your Workbook.

For which ones do you need a turning force?

Compare your **answers** with your group.

Which do you agree on?

Which do you not agree on?

Why are your answers different?

WB 59

3 Forces at work

Your teacher has put objects around the room.

Try each object.

What kind of force do you need to make it work?

Can you use more than one force for any of the objects?

Tell the rest of the class about what you found.

Draw one object in your Workbook.

WB 60

4 Faster and slower

Some movements are fast. Some movements are slow.

Look at the pairs of pictures in your Workbook.

Which movement in each pair is faster or slower?

WB 60

Interesting fact

Did you know that biting is a force? Scientists can measure how strong a bite is. A hyena's bite is about six times stronger than a human bite. Ouch!

Making it fast and making it slow

If you push a toy car, it will move. It can be made to go faster or slower.

Look at the picture.

Predict a way to make the car go faster.

Predict a way to make the car go slower.

Hint

When you predict, you say what you think is going to happen.

Forces and movement

Forces can make things move. But sometimes the thing does not move, even if we push or pull very hard.

5 Can you make it move?

Push against a big tree. Does the tree move?

Now pull on a rope tied to the tree. Does the tree move now?

Look at the tug of war. The boys are both pulling, but no one is moving.

Why do you think this happens?

WB 61

Extension

What force is the woman using to put the boxes in the van?

What force could she use if she had no trolley?

Do you think it is easier moving the boxes with a trolley?

Why?

WB 61

Checklist

Complete these statements on page 62 of your Workbook.

- I can talk about different kinds of force.
- I can say what forces do.
- I know that pushes and pulls are kinds of force.

4.3 Speeding up and slowing down

In this section, I am learning:

- to see changes in movement
- what makes movement change.

Key words

cause, faster, fastest, friction, share, slower, slowest, stop, watch

Watch a weight swinging on a string.

What happens to the movement as it swings?

Changing movement

The picture shows cyclists on a track.

They are changing direction as they go round.

They go **faster** after the start.

They go **slower** before they **stop**.

1 The bicycle ride

Look at the picture. It shows a bicycle ride.

- Where does the bicycle speed up?
- Where does the bicycle slow down?
- Where does the bicycle change direction?

Draw your own roads on a big piece of paper.

Use a toy bicycle to go to the shop.

WB 63

Movement outside

2 What makes things move outside?

Look at the leaves outside. Are they moving?

Blow some bubbles. Can you make the bubbles move?

Look at a flag. Is it moving?

In a group, play a game to keep a balloon in the air.

What makes these things move?

Hint

The air moves.

You can feel the air move on a windy day.

WB 63

More moving things

Forces can make things move. They **cause** the movement.

When something speeds up, a force is making it go faster. The force is the cause.

When something slows down, a force is making it go slower. The force is the cause.

When something changes direction, a force is making it go in a different way. The force is the cause.

Extension

It is not always easy to make a thing move by pushing or pulling.

Gently push a big book across a table. What do you feel?

Gently push the book across a carpet. How does it feel different?

Hint

When something moves against something else it creates a force. This force is called **friction**. It slows the movement down.

WB 64

3 Rolling marbles

Use chalk to draw a circle on the ground.

Stand five steps away.

Gently roll a marble towards the circle.

Talk with your partner. Describe the movement you see.

Try to get the marble to stop in the circle.

What kinds of force are at work? **Share** your ideas with your partner.

WB 64

4 Changing speed

Try again to get the marble in the circle. This time use a ramp.

How did you use the ramp?

Look what the marble does.

- When is the marble **fastest**?
- When is the marble **slowest**?

WB 65

Interesting fact

The force from the wind can make things move very fast. Watch a video clip of a sailing boat.

Checklist

Complete these statements on page 66 of your Workbook.

- I can see changes in movement.
- I can compare speeding up and slowing down.
- I can talk about what makes movement change.

What have I learnt?

Answer these questions on the worksheet your teacher gives you.

1 Look at the pictures.
Where can you see these forces?

pushing | pulling | turning

2 Choose a word from the box to complete each sentence.

jump | wind | turning | swinging

- The _____ makes a flag wave.
- A frog can _____ high.
- When I hang onto a branch and move forwards and backwards, I am _____.
- When a car moves, its wheels are _____.

3 What action words can you use to describe how the girl and the car move?

4 How can the father make the girl swing a little bit?

How can he make the swing go higher?

How can he stop the girl swinging?

5 Making sounds

In this unit, I am learning:

- where sounds come from
- what different sounds are like
- that sounds can be loud or soft
- what makes sounds loud or soft
- how a sound changes when I move towards or away from it
- that we hear when sound enters our ears
- what loud sounds do to my hearing
- how to protect my hearing
- about using hearing to stay safe.

Key words

ear hear
loud safe
soft sound

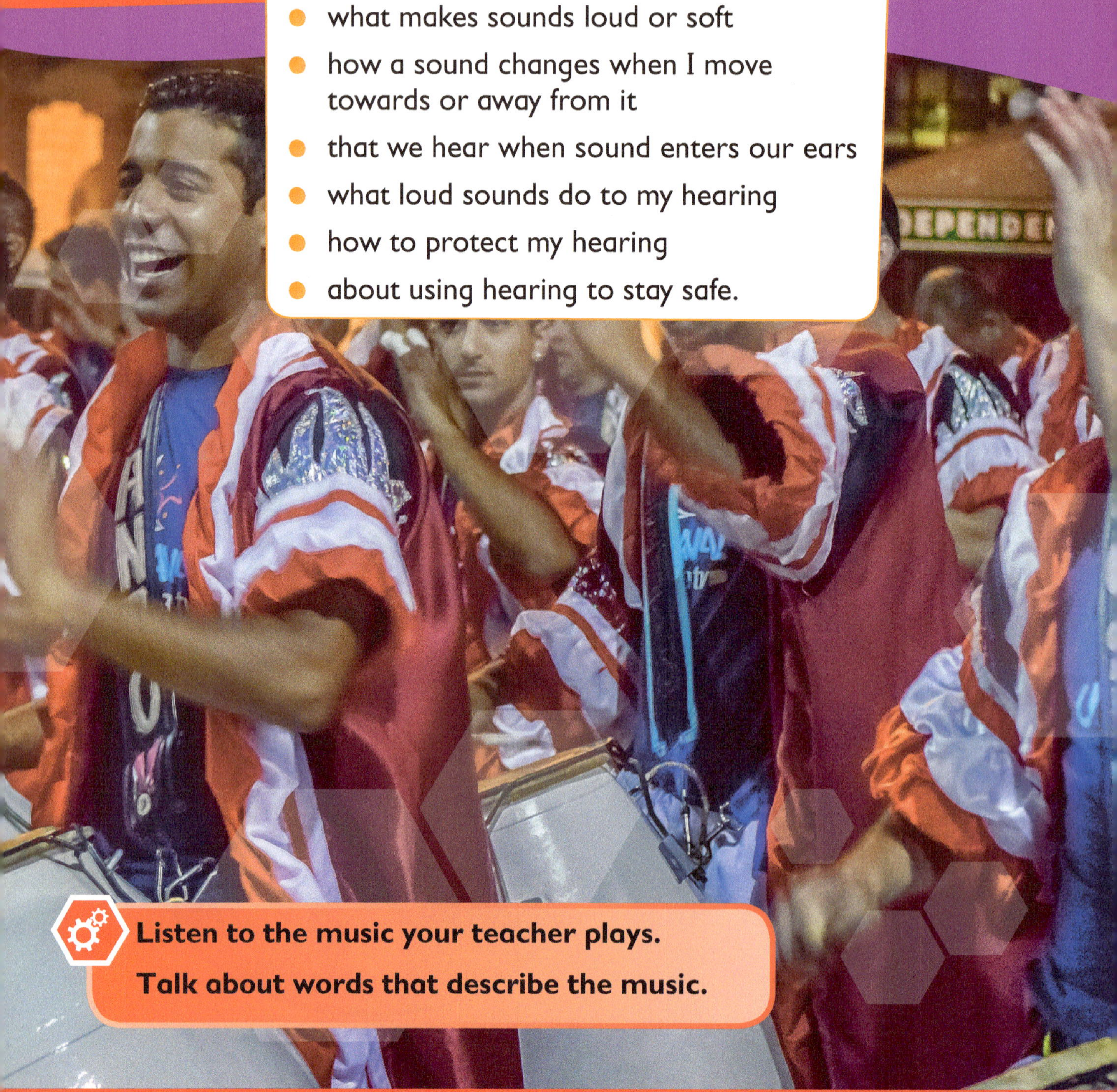

Listen to the music your teacher plays.
Talk about words that describe the music.

5.1 Where does sound come from?

In this section, I am learning:

- where sounds come from
- what different sounds are like.

Key words

ask	compare
draw	guess
hear	hearing
listen	look
name	sound
tell	voice

What makes a sound?

Working as a class, name as many sounds as you can.

Look at the pictures – do they give you extra ideas?

What sounds do these things make?

Making sounds

Sounds come from many places.

Many actions make sounds.

1 Making sounds

What sounds can you make with your **voice**? Try making:

- scary sounds
- funny sounds
- gentle sounds

What sounds can you make in other ways?

- Clap your hands.
- Snap your fingers.
- Slap your thighs.

Now, sing a song about sound as a class. **Draw** some of your actions.

WB 68

2 Finding sounds

Your teacher has put many things around the room that make sounds.
Try each one.
How did you make sounds with them?

WB 70

3 Animal sounds

Your teacher will play you some animal sounds.

Listen to the sounds.

Guess what the animal is.

Why do animals make sounds?

Compare ideas with your partner.

WB 71

Hearing is a sense

You already know that **hearing** is one of our senses.

We use our ears to **hear**.

Hearing can **tell** you about things you cannot see or touch.

4 Mystery tins

Your teacher will give you tins with something inside.

Do not **look** inside.

Make sounds using each tin.

What is inside?

Do you need to **ask** for help?

WB 71

Hint

You can make sounds by hitting, rubbing and shaking.

Extension

A guitar can make different sounds.
Try it.
What sounds can you make?

WB 72

What might the world be like without sound?

Interesting fact

Some animals have very good hearing.

Bats can hear sounds that humans cannot. Their sense of hearing helps them fly safely in the dark.

Checklist

Complete these statements on page 72 of your Workbook.

- I can say where sounds come from.
- I can tell different sounds apart.
- I can use words to say what different sounds are like.

5.2 Loud and soft

In this section, I am learning:

- that sounds can be loud or soft
- what makes sounds loud or soft
- how a sound changes when I move towards or away from it.

Key words

far, find, loud, louder, near, quiet, show, sirens, soft

Look at the pictures. What sounds do these things make?

Loud sounds and soft sounds

Your teacher will play a musical instrument.

The sounds can be **soft**.

The sounds can be **loud**.

Playing gently makes soft sounds.

Playing harder makes **louder** sounds.

1 Making loud and soft sounds

Work in pairs. Take it in turns to make loud and soft sounds.

- Clap your hands gently. Then clap your hands hard.
- Whisper a message. Then shout a message.

WB 73

Sounds from far and near

Sounds can be heard when they are **near**. They can also be heard from **far** away.

2 Listening carefully

Be **quiet** and stand at the back of the room.

Listen. Can you hear the sound?

Move a little closer. Can you hear the sound now?

WB 73

3 Listening in pairs

Get into pairs.

Can you hear a whisper?

Can you hear it from a distance?

Let's **find** out.

WB 74

Hint

When a sound is near, it sounds louder than when it is far away.

Emergency sounds

Police cars, fire engines and ambulances have **sirens**. The sound of a siren tells us about an emergency.

Look at the picture. What is happening?

Do you think the fire engine's siren is loud or soft?

Tell your partner why you say so.

4 Travelling sound

Your teacher will **show** you a video.

Listen as the emergency vehicle comes closer and then moves away again.

When was the sound louder? When was the sound softer?

Unscramble the words about sound in your Workbook.

WB 74

5 Word whispers

Play a game.

Look at the sound words here.

crash snap ring pop

Sit or stand in a line with your group.

Whisper one word to the person next to you.

Each person whispers it to the next.

The last person writes the word down. Did they get it right?

WB 75

Interesting fact

Sounds can travel underwater. Whales make sounds to send messages to each other underwater.

✓ Checklist

Complete these statements on page 75 of your Workbook.

- I know the difference between loud and soft sounds.
- I can describe some soft sounds and some loud sounds.
- I know how to make loud and soft sounds.
- I can say what happens to a sound when I move towards or away from it.

5.3 Protecting my hearing

In this section, I am learning:

- that we hear when sound enters our ears
- what loud sounds do to my hearing
- how to protect my hearing
- about using hearing to stay safe.

Key words

damage
ear
protect
safe
write

Some students in the class cannot hear.

Who is helping them understand what the teacher is saying?

What sense do they use instead?

When someone cannot hear, they use their other senses more.

1 What can you hear?

Your teacher will play you some sounds.

Cover both your ears.

Now listen with only one **ear**.

Then listen with both ears.

Now use pieces of cloth to cover both of your ears. What do you notice?

WB 76

How safe is this?

Many people get injured near roads.

We need our senses to help us stay **safe**.

2 ### Staying safe

Look at the picture.

What can you tell the person to help her stay safe?

Discuss your idea in a group.

WB 77

Protecting your hearing

Loud sounds can **damage** your hearing.

Ear defenders **protect** your ears from loud sounds.

Why is this person wearing ear defenders?

3 ### Make your own ear defenders

Omar and Alec are going to visit a building site.

They need ear defenders.

Work in a group. Think about how to make some ear defenders.

WB 77

You can protect your hearing by:

- not playing music very loudly
- never putting things into your ears
- wearing ear protection in places where you will hear very loud sounds.

Extension

The truck makes a very loud sound.
What sounds are not as loud as the truck?
Write them in your Workbook.

WB 78

Checklist

Complete these statements on page 79 of your Workbook.

- I know that we hear sound when it enters our ears.
- I can say what can damage my hearing.
- I can say how to protect my hearing.
- I can say how hearing can help keep me safe.

What have I learnt?

Answer these questions on the worksheet your teacher gives you.

1. How loud are these?

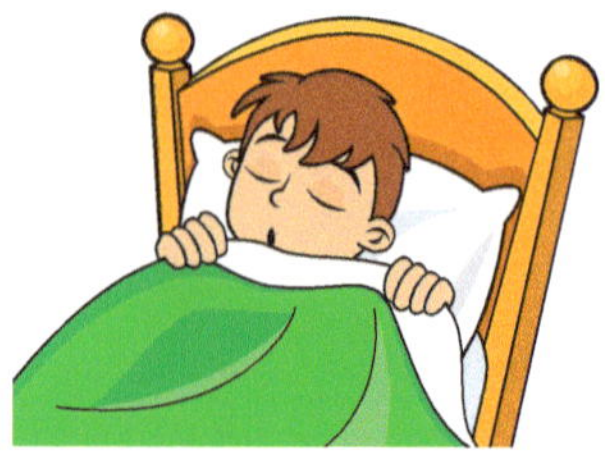

2. Three children are listening to the truck.

Which statements about the picture are correct?

- The truck will sound the same to all three children.
- The truck will sound loudest to Amina.
- The truck will sound softest to Kim.
- The truck will sound softest to David.

3. What do you hear if you walk away from a sound?

4. Which sentences are true?

- Ear defenders make it easier to hear someone talking.
- Ear defenders protect your hearing from loud noises.
- You should wear ear defenders when you are walking to school.

6 Growing plants

In this unit, I am learning:

- about the parts of a plant
- about different kinds of plant
- about seeds
- how to grow plants from seeds
- how to make a prediction
- that plants need water to live and grow
- that plants need light to live and grow
- how to do a fair test.

Key words

fair test
grow
light
plant
seed
water

Look at the picture.

How many different kinds of plant can you see?

6.1 Parts of a plant

In this section, I am learning:

- about the parts of a plant
- about different kinds of plant.

Key words

draw
flower
leaf
leaves
plant
roots
stem
tell

Find a plant that you can study closely. What can you see?

Use a magnifying glass to look at a part of the plant more closely.

The main parts of a plant

Plants have **roots**, **leaves** and a **stem**.

Sometimes plants have **flowers**.

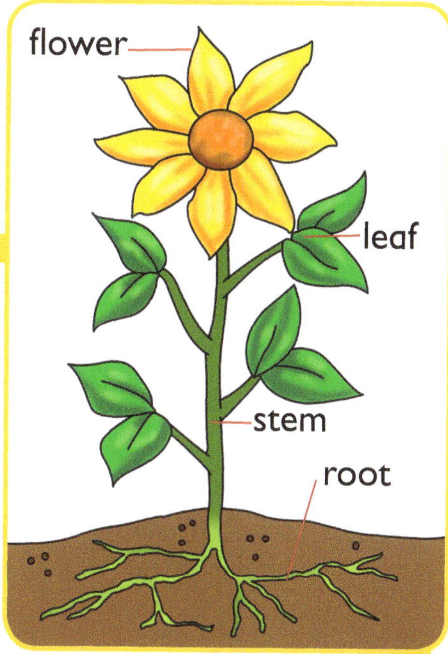

1 Naming the parts of a plant

Look at a **plant**.

Point to the different parts on the plant.

What part is under the soil?

Say the name of each part.

Draw the plant in your Workbook. Label the parts.

WB 81

Different kinds of plant

2 Different plants

Look outside for plants.

How many different kinds can you see?

Look at grass and a tree.

What is the same? What is different?

WB 81

Hint

Trees have roots, stems, leaves and sometimes flowers.

They are also plants.

3 Making a model plant

Work in a group. Make a model of a plant.

Make a display.

WB 83

Look at these two plants. They do not look the same.

But they both have the same parts.

They are both alive.

Extension

How can you **tell** that plants are alive?

What can living things do that non-living things cannot do?

WB 83

Interesting fact

The tallest tree in the world is a giant redwood. It is taller than 60 people.

What would the world be like without plants?

Checklist

Complete these statements on page 84 of your Workbook.

- I can name the parts of a plant.
- I know about different types of plant.

6.2 Where do plants come from?

In this section, I am learning:

- about seeds
- how to grow plants from seeds
- how to make a prediction.

Key words

ask
grow
guess
predict
seeds
share
water

Look at the picture. What is happening? Talk about it in your group.

Seeds

Adult plants make **seeds**.

Seeds come in many shapes and sizes.

All seeds do the same job. Their job is to **grow** into new plants.

1 Looking at seeds

Look at the seeds your teacher gives you.

Draw the seeds. Describe them.

WB 85

Extension

Make a display using seeds.

WB 85

Life keeps itself going

A seed grows into a new plant.

The adult plant grows flowers.

The flowers make seeds.

The seeds grow into more new plants.

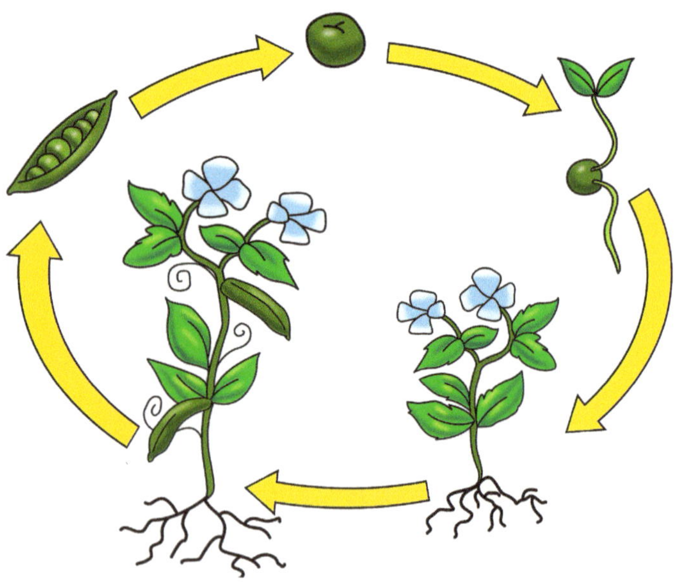

2 Ordering pictures

Look at the pictures in your Workbook. They show the stages in a plant's life.

Work out the correct order of the pictures.

WB 86

3 Watching how a seed grows

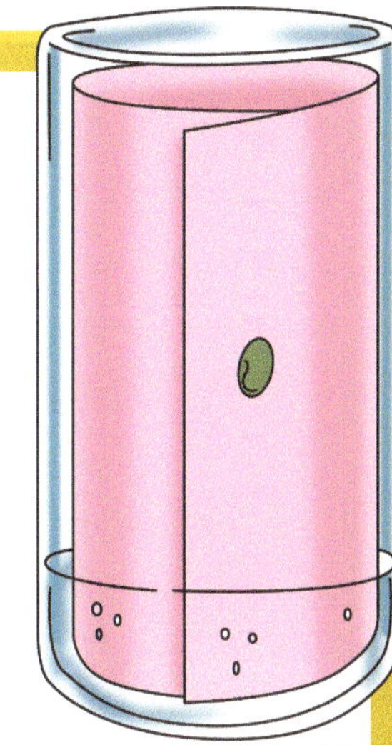

Trap a seed against the side of a jar with moist blotting paper. Make sure there is some **water** in the jar.

Put the jar in a dark place.

Can you **guess** or **predict** what will happen?

Draw what you see after a few days.

Make sure you show all the parts you can see.

Label the parts.

WB 86

Can you predict how this plant came to be here? How do you think it started growing?

4 Growing plants from seeds

You can grow plants from seeds. Follow these steps:

1 Put some soil in a pot.

2 Put a few seeds on top.

3 Sprinkle a bit of soil on top.

4 Water the seeds a little every day.

Draw what you see after 10 days. Keep watering the new plant every day. How big is the plant after another week?

WB 87

Interesting fact

Seeds that are hundreds of years old can start to grow if they have the right things.

Date palms like this have grown from 2000-year-old seeds.

5 Thinking about seeds

Sit quietly.

Think of three things you have learnt about seeds.

Tell your partner. **Ask** them what they have learnt.

WB 88

Learn this song as a class. **Share** it with someone at home.

Jared's seed song (tune of "Twinkle, twinkle, little star")

Bread and rice are made from seeds
Spread some seeds and birds will feed
Plant your seeds and they will grow
We did this and we can show
How a plant comes from a seed
A tree, a flower or a weed.

✓ Checklist

Complete these statements on page 88 of your Workbook.

- I know that seeds grow into new plants.
- I can predict why seeds grow.
- I know that seeds need water to start growing.

6.3 What plants need

In this section, I am learning:

- that plants need water to live and grow
- that plants need light to live and grow
- how to do a fair test.

Key words

answer
compare
fair test
light
write

Look at a collection of plants.

Do you think the plants look healthy?

What do plants need to stay alive?

1 Growing healthy plants

Use two plants that are the same.

Water one plant every day for one week.

Do not water the other plant.

Compare the two plants.

WB 89

Hint

Plants can live for a while without being watered. Plants have water inside them.

Extension

Start watering both plants.

Look at the plants as often as you can over the next two days.

What changes do you see?

WB 89

What do plants need to grow?

We can find out what plants need to grow. To find out, we have to do a **fair test**.

In a fair test we compare two things that are the same. But we treat these two things differently. The two treatments may differ in only one way. Everything else must be the same.

A fair test can compare plants that are watered with plants that are not watered. The test you did in Activity 1 was a fair test.

2 Doing a fair test: Do plants need light?

You need two young plants of the same type.

Make sure both plants have water.

Keep one in a dark place. Keep one in a **light** place.

Compare the plants every day.

What did you find out from your test?

In your Workbook, **answer** the questions and **write** why this is a fair test.

WB 90

All living things need food.

Where do plants get their food?

Interesting fact

On a forest floor the light is dim. Some plants can grow even where the light is dim.

3 Remembering what you learnt

Sometimes an image can help us remember what we learnt.

Complete the sentences in your Workbook.

What shape do the sentences form?

WB 91

Checklist

Complete these statements on page 91 of your Workbook.

- I know that plants need water to live and grow.
- I know that plants need light to live and grow.
- I can do a fair test.

What have I learnt?

Answer these questions on the worksheet your teacher gives you.

1. Name the parts of the plant.

   Name two other parts not shown in the picture.

2. Compare the plants in the picture.

What is the same for the two plants?

What is different for the two plants?

3. Which sentences are correct?

Plants are living things.

Seeds need light to start growing.

Trees are plants.

Seeds need water to start growing.

Glossary

alive	Describes a living thing that is still breathing, growing, moving or feeding.
animal	A living creature that eats and moves around on its own.
answer	To speak or write something when someone asks you a question.
arms	The body parts that connect the hands and wrists to the shoulders.
artificial	Describes something that is made by people but looks or works like something found in nature.
ask	To make a request or seek an answer to a question.
bendy	Describes something that is soft and flexible.
body	All the parts of a person or an animal.
cause	To make something happen.
choose	To pick something from a group.
cold	Without warmth.
compare	To see how something is the same as or different from something else.
damage	To harm, injure or break something.
damp	Slightly wet.
dead	Describes a living thing that can no longer breathe, grow, move or feed.
different	Not the same.
draw	To make a picture with a pen or pencil.
drink	To swallow a liquid.
dry	Without water.
ear	The organ with which animals hear.
eat	To put food into the mouth, chew and swallow.
eyes	The organs with which animals see.
fabric	A soft material woven or knitted from threads.
fair test	An investigation to compare two of the same things treated differently in only one way; all the other things in the test stay the same.
family	A group of adults and children who are related or live together.
far	A long distance away.
farm	An area of land used to grow crops or keep animals for food and clothing.
fast	Happening quickly or with great speed.
faster	Happening more quickly or with greater speed than something else.

fastest	To be the quickest.
feet (foot)	Body parts at the end of the legs on which the body stands.
find	To discover something after searching.
find out	To discover or explore something.
fingers	The parts of the body found at the end of each hand.
flower	The part of a plant where seeds are made.
foam	A soft, artificial material that feels like a sponge.
food	Anything that is used by living things to give them energy and to help them grow.
food groups	Collections of foods that all do the same job in the body.
friction	A force that slows movement when one thing moves against another.
force	A push or a pull on an object to make it move, slow down, change direction or change shape.
generation	A group of people who were born around the same time.
glass	A hard, shiny material that you can see through.
group	A collection of people or things that are all together in one place.
grow	To become taller or larger.
guess	To give an answer without having much information.
hair	Thin, soft threads that grow from the skin of humans and some animals.
hands	Body parts at the end of the arms used for grasping or holding.
hard	Describes an object or material that cannot easily be broken, cut or squashed.
head	The top part of the body, containing the brain, eyes, ears, nose and mouth.
healthy	(1) Describes something that is good for your health. (2) To be free from sickness.
hear	To receive sound through the ears.
hearing	The sense used to pick up sound.
human	A person.
job	A task something or someone does.
jump	To leap into the air.
knees	The joints between the upper legs and lower legs, allowing the legs to bend.
leaf	The part of a plant that grows from the stem or a branch.
leaves	The plural of leaf.
legs	Parts of the lower body used for walking, running and jumping.
light	A form of energy that can be seen.
listen	To pay attention when hearing a sound.
living	Describes something that is or once has been alive.
look	To deliberately focus the eyes on something.
loud	Describes a sound that can easily be heard.
louder	Describes a sound that can easily be heard further away.

mammal An animal that feeds on its mother's milk.

material What something is made from.

metal A hard material that usually looks shiny and makes a ringing sound when struck.

mouth The opening in the face through which an animal or human eats, breathes or makes a sound.

move To change position.

movement, moving The act of changing position.

name To say the word by which something is known.

near A short distance away.

non-living Describes something that does not live or has never been alive.

nose The body part used by some animals, including humans, to breathe and smell.

nylon A material made by humans that is strong, light and long-lasting.

object Anything that has a shape or form and can be seen or touched.

paper A thin material made by pressing wood pulp into flat sheets.

pet A tame animal kept in the home for fun or company.

plant A living thing that has roots, a stem and leaves and needs light and water to live.

plastic A strong, light material made by humans that can be easily shaped when warm and soft; it can be hard or soft when it cools.

polystyrene Light, stiff foam used for packing, for protecting fragile objects or to make moulded products such as cups.

predict To suggest what might happen in the future based on what you already know.

properties A word used to describe what makes a material or object look, feel or behave as it does.

protect To keep something from being harmed.

pull A force that brings something closer.

push A force that moves something away.

quiet Making no or very little sound.

real Describes something that actually exists or is alive.

roots The parts of a plant that hold it in the soil and grow downwards, taking in water and nutrients from the ground.

rubber A stretchy, bendy material.

safe Free from risk or harm.

same Describes things that are identical.

say To speak.

see To become aware of something by using your eyes.

seeds The part of a flowering plant that grows into a new plant.

senses The systems through which humans and animals become aware of what is going on around them, namely sight, hearing, touch, smell and taste.

share To divide up or give out something.

shoulders The part of the body between the neck and upper arm.

show To give something to someone to look at.

sight The ability to see.

similar Almost the same but not identical.

sirens Something that makes a loud warning sound.

slow Not happening quickly.

slower Not as fast as something else.

slowest Describes the thing with the least speed.

smell The sense used to detect odours.

soft Easy to squash or bend.

sort To organise or divide things into groups.

sound Anything that people or animals can hear with their ears.

stem The part of a plant that grows upright and supports the leaves.

stone A hard, natural material that comes from the ground and is used for building or carving.

stop To no longer move or do something; to end.

strong Describes objects that cannot easily break.

swing To move forwards and backwards.

talk about To discuss or share information with others.

taste The ability to notice flavour.

tell To say something to someone.

toes Parts of the body found at the end of each foot.

touch (feel) To become aware of something using the skin.

turn To move along a curve.

voice The sounds made with your mouth and throat.

watch To look at or observe with attention.

water The most common liquid on Earth and essential to life.

waterproof Not letting water through.

wood The hard material found underneath the bark of a tree trunk, often used to make furniture.

write To record information on paper using a pen or pencil.

young Baby animals.